Basingstoke

in old picture postcards

by
Robert Brown

European Library – Zaltbommel/Netherlands

GB ISBN 90 288 5258 1 / CIP

© 1991 European Library – Zaltbommel/Netherlands

INTRODUCTION

Basingstoke, tucked away in the fold of the Loddon Valley, is situated in the north-east of Hampshire. The River Loddon rises to the west of the town and flows across the countryside to the River Thames.

The town has its origins from the early Mesolithic settlers of some 7,000 years ago, and since then its unique position in southern England has been used by people of all types from the Celts to the Romans to establish an encampment of much importance. When the Basinga tribe came to the area in the 8th century they built a protective stockade around their huts and called it the 'Basinga's Stoc'. Thus Basingstoke was born. The Domesday Book of 1086 quotes the town as a Royal Manor and mentions that the occupants had never paid any taxes. The parish church of St. Michael is also referred to, although the present building was mainly built in the 16th century.

The market, which originates from the 13th century, was held on a Sunday but later changed to Monday and then Wednesday. An additional market is now held on Saturdays. Goods and animals were sold in front of the old Mote Hall in the Market Square until a cattle market was established near the railway station in 1873. This closed down in 1966 to make way for the Town Development Scheme.

The roads of the town were established in the medieval days, with two tracks leading down to the lower part of Basingstoke on either side of the Market Square, while roads to London and Winchester went their opposite ways. Further tracks branched off to the various nearby towns and villages, allowing wagons and other vehicles to transport their goods to the area.

On the Liten Hill, to the north of the town, the Holy Ghost Guild built their chapel in the 15th century and the ruins remain close to the railway station.

A series of disasters in the 17th century led to the town's trade being hit badly, including fires, the plague, and the Civil War ravages at nearby Basing House. But by 1724, when the author Daniel Defoe came to the town, during his travels, Basingstoke was on the road to recovery and prosperity.

At the end of the 18th century the construction of the Basingstoke Canal brought the town further trade, which prospered until the arrival of the railway in 1839. By the 1860's business had declined so much on the Canal that it was forced to close down at the Basingstoke end. Then the railway took over its business.

The Victorian period saw many social changes in the town, including the construction of the Gasworks, the building of a new Town Hall, and the opening of a Corn Exchange. Commercial and industrial firms opened up in the town, while the outlying fields were purchased for residential purposes in the 1880's.

When Queen Victoria came to the throne in 1837 the population of Basingstoke was nearly 4,000. When she died in 1901 it had increased to 9,510 — more than double.

During the Edwardian period Basingstoke was to realise that the increase in road transport, through the invention of the combustion engine, was to bring more trade to the town. It also brought a good deal of traffic as well, and attempts at reducing the dust, or mud, whatever the weather, led to better and wider roads.

As the population grew, better services and facilities were provided, including entertainment. Theatrical and cinematic enjoyment by the local folk was joined by other forms of social activities, due to people having more time with their families. In the 1930's a series of carnivals brought the spirit of fun to the town, the money collected being put toward a new hospital planned close to the one built in 1879. Unfortunately the Second World War brought a halt to the idea.

During the war the town was hit on several occasions by enemy bombs, and in August 1940 three fell within yards of each other causing considerable damage and killing many people. Within a decade of the war ending the scars had been healed, and thoughts of development in the town were becoming a reality. In 1952 an Act of Parliament was to realise within ten years the Town Development Plan, which was to bring thousands of people from the London area to Basingstoke. To allow this expansion of the town, drastic alterations had to be carried out, including the demolition of most of the town centre, the clearance of residential areas, road closures, and reconstruction of certain public services. The demolition of the greater part of the town centre, in 1966-1968, caused much inconvenience for a time, and led to the disappearance of many fine and ancient buildings which had stood the test of time for centuries. Many of the little shops which had given the town its character were removed, with offices, churches, cottages, a school, a cinema, and other buildings. In their place a concrete shopping centre and multi-storey car park were built, the first phase being opened in late 1968.

Meanwhile new housing, industrial and commercial estates were being erected around the town, while a new road system was laid out to cope with the increase in traffic. During the period of development the population increased from 25,950 to 80,000.

The new Basingstoke has much to attract people from far and near with sporting facilities, entertainment complexes, a ring road system, a large shopping area with many of the High Street stores contained within it, and many organisations, clubs, and societies throughout the area.

But although the town has been drastically altered in recent years, there is still a hint of the old left in various places. Old buildings, old names, and old streets can be found around Basingstoke, preserving the antiquity which used to prevail not so many years ago. It is hoped that the pictures in this book will illustrate how the town used to look like. Have a nice journey into the past!

My grateful thanks to Mrs. Dorothy Locke for the use of some of her old photographs of Basingstoke.

Robert Brown

PICTURES OF DAYS GONE BY

Nostalgia reflects from the pages,
Pictures of days gone by;
Different times and distant ages
Caught with the camera's eye.

Peaceful scenes of quiet places,
A country scene in days of old;
Past remembered, names and faces
Do photographs unfold.

Without these pictures who would know
The Basingstoke that used to be,
These ageing photographs that show
Time captured for eternity.

Poem published by permission of Maureen Barfoot.

1. The corner of Market Place and London Street before its demolition in 1872. The site was originally a warehouse kept by Mr. Aburrow, and even after his nephew took over the business it was still called Aburrow's Corner. In later years the corner was acquired by Timothy Whites and Taylors, the chemists, then about twenty years ago it was demolished and rebuilt into the present Rent Office, and various shops.

2. Winchester Street in the mid-19th century, showing part of the 16th century old Angel Inn in the Market Place. The Angel, used by most of the stage-coaches that passed through the town, was closed for business on 1st March 1866. A few weeks later it was sold by auction and among the many items on display were 11 cab horses, 17 prime feather beds and a four-post bed, 40 barrels of old ale, two circular fronted broughams, and two omnibuses. The building consisted of bedrooms, sitting-rooms, coffee rooms, commercial rooms, a bar, a smoking room, a dairy, and a kitchen.

3. The corner of Church Street and Brook Street in the mid-19th century. The buildings were part of the Merton Farm, which stood on the site of the medieval St. John's Hospital, founded in the 13th century by Walter de Merton for old and infirm priests. The farm was built on this land in 1778 to allow the animals to use the nearby River Loddon for drinking purposes. In 1888 the farm moved to the Aldermaston Road and the site was acquired for a school and various businesses. In 1967 the area was demolished for town development purposes.

4. Winton Square in the late Victorian times, on the Winton House side. Winton Square received its name from this house, which was once a ladies boarding school. Later it became the offices of the Post Office telephone section, and was badly damaged by a serious fire early this year. The large house in the picture became the site for Mr. Edney's furniture store after this area was demolished and rebuilt in 1907. In the centre of the square there used to be a horse trough, but this was removed in the 1950's.

5. The railway station in the late 19th century, when there were only two lines running through the town. Built in 1839, the station was rebuilt in 1904 to take an extra two lines for trains travelling on the southern line, which cost some £30,000. This also meant that bridges along the track had to be altered and extended, such as the Chapel Street and Reading Road bridges, which meant a great deal of disruption to traffic.

6. The fields of Eastrop parish, to the East of Basingstoke. Where Eastfield Avenue and the roads of the Riverdene housing estate are, was once farmland belonging to the Goldings Farm, which was part of the large Goldings estate of which the War Memorial Park is now on the site of. In the distance is the Church of St. Mary, the parish church of Eastrop, which was rebuilt in 1886. The church register dates back to 1750. Eastrop extended to other areas at one time, including the Hackwood Park, but in the 1890's borough boundary changes confined it to the town.

7. Members of the Basingstoke Cricket Club outside their original thatched pavilion in the late 19th century. In 1901 a new pavilion was erected on land at Bounty Road, which became known as May's Bounty, after John May who provided the finance to stop the building of houses on the site and to allow the Club to flourish. The field, originally known as the Folly, was enlarged to its present size over the following years, and the pavilion was extended. The cricket club dates back to 1817 when it is recorded that a Basingstoke team was formed in the town. In 1901 it became the Basingstoke and North Hants Cricket Club, under which name it still exists.

8. The scene in Winchester Street after a fire at the premises of Mr. Jacobs, the printer and general stationer, some time in the late 19th century. The building was once the general store and Post Office kept by Robert Cottle between 1808 and 1859. Outside the store, inserted in the wall, was placed the first postbox in Basingstoke, and this was preserved when structural alterations were made in later years. The building is still there and now holds a baker's shop and an electrical shop.

9. John Hacker, the local Beadle, in the 1870's. Mr. Hacker, a beer retailer who lived in Hackwood Road, was the parish officer for Basingstoke, a position which included duties such as mace bearer, town crier, and assistant to the constable. Mr. Hacker also kept the 'Flower Pots', a public house, on the west side of Hackwood Road, which was burnt down after the thatch caught fire in 1864. It was never rebuilt.

10. Sarum Hill in the late 19th century, looking up the hill toward Winton Square. The New Inn was one of several new public houses at that time, which were built to cater for an increase in the town's population. With the construction of the houses along Essex Road and those of George Street, Alexandra Road and Queens Road, the inn was well patronised. In more recent years the New Inn has been altered and added to.

11. London Street in the 1880's, looking towards the Market Place. The road surface was far from perfect due to constant use by waggons and horses, this being the main road through the town. In Elizabethan days this road was known as Bower Street, some of the buildings still having traces of that time. The left hand side, opposite the United Reform Church, has retained several of the original buildings, including the old Jacob's Alley. The right hand building is now Butler's mens outfitters, but was once a baker's shop with ovens at the rear.

12. Hillside House in Vyne Road after being damaged by the Massaganian group in the early 1880's. When the Salvation Army was established in the town in 1880 there was a great deal of aggression against them by the Publicans and Brewery owners due to their cry of 'Ban all drink'. In the midst of all the 'battles' of those days a local election brought about further strife, resulting in a running fight with the police through the town and up to Southview, with many shops and houses having their windows broken. Businessmen such as Mr. J.B. Soper, the foundry owner, at Hillside House, were also hit.

13. Downsland House, off Worting Road, at the turn of the century, showing the family and staff posing for a picture. The house was part of the small Downsland Estate, which adjoined the Bramblys Grange Estate. When the land was purchased in the 1930's for building purposes the house was made into flats, and private houses were gradually built along the old driveway, which is now Downsland Road. This track was eventually made into a solid road in 1965. Also in the 1930's a parade of shops was built on the Worting Road side of the land. Downsland House was demolished in 1974 and replaced by a block of maisonettes called Lisa Court.

Messrs. SALTER & WYATT, Architects, LONDON.

14. The Corn Exchange in upper Wote Street, after being opened in February 1865. Built at a cost of nearly £5,000 it was used by farmers from all over Hampshire and Berkshire. By 1890 it boasted of some 150 stands for all types of cattle and other animals. The enlargement of the cattle market by the railway station, after its opening in 1873, led to most business being transferred to there, and the Corn Exchange was used for other purposes, such as dances, a skating rink, and a theatre. During its use as a cinema it was burnt down in 1925, and later rebuilt. It is now the Haymarket Theatre.

15. Fairfields School at the turn of the century. Built in the mid-1880's it was opened in February 1888 for 1,300 children, having been established by a School Board formed in 1885. Built at a cost of £12,000, the average attendance was 329 boys, 294 girls, and 185 infants by 1911. When the Board School was opened pupils from most of the small schools in the town were marched up the roads to Fairfields to take their place in the classrooms. The school bell used to toll its daily message, but upon the outbreak of war in 1939 it was never rung again. The stone crowns on the roof were removed for safety reasons.

16. Winchester Street at the turn of the century, looking west towards Winton Square. On the right is the entrance to Joice's Yard, which once held a coach-building business and was originally the yard of the Crown Inn. Opposite is the original shoe shop of Alfred Milward, who later established the large chain of shops all over the country, having begun his business in 1857. The buildings in this road have mainly stayed the same in structure, although further down fires and alterations have changed the scene.

17. The Pear Tree Inn, in Flaxfield Road, in the 1890's. This old posting house was later rebuilt to a different design, then demolished in the 1960's for the construction of Timberlake Road. This was one of several public houses in Flaxfield Road, which gave the town its popular tag of 'a pub every few yards' in the Victorian and Edwardian eras. Church Lane, which led down to the parish church of St. Michael's, was by the side of the Pear Tree, and the local vicar of that time often said that it was a short route to all those who wanted to abstain.

HACKWOOD. PARK.

18. Hackwood Park lodge in the late Victorian period. This large private estate south of Basingstoke was once the home of Lord Curzon, and of the members of the Belgian Royal Family during the Great War. The park, which boasts of much wild life both of plant and animal, is skirted by a long flint and brick wall on the Alton Road side. Hackwood Road in Basingstoke is named after the park, although at one time it was called Duke Street after the Duke of Bolton, the owner of the park. Hackwood Park was well-known for its avenues of trees, such as Paradise Walk and 'the Cathedral', but the hurricane winds of recent years have caused considerable damage to them.

19. Station Hill in the 1870's just prior to the construction of the clothing factory of Gerrish, Ames, and Simpkins in 1878. This road, which led from lower Wote Street up to the railway station, was one of the steepest in the town and the local folk were pleased, when climbing it, that there was a café near the top where they could have a rest and a cup of tea. For those who preferred something stronger, the Station Hotel was at the top of the hill, next to the station. Wallis and Haslam, built in 1860, later became Wallis and Steevens. They manufactured agricultural vehicles and other equipment until the factory was demolished in 1966 for the Town Development Scheme. They moved to new premises at Daneshill but closed down a few years later.

20. Chapel Street in the late Victorian period, showing the 17th century houses on the west side which were demolished in the 1960's. The houses in the distance were pulled down in 1901 to make way for the Railway Goods Yard entrance. The yard was in use for some eighty years until it was sold for office use. Chapel Street was originally called Whitewaye, but the nearby presence of the Holy Ghost Chapel brought the change of name.

21. New Street at the turn of the century. This road, once called Stew Lane, was a diversion to Church Street via Cross Street, and a route to the top of Flaxfield Road. John Mares' clothing factory was half way down New Street, on the right, which remained in business until the late 1950's. The shops on the left were gradually taken over by the Co-operative Society, then in 1960 they were demolished to make way for a large store for the firm. This in turn was demolished in 1985 for the erection of an office block.

22. Soper's Grove at Southview in the 1880's, during the development of the area. With the gradual expansion of the town came the inevitable intrusion into the outer areas of Basingstoke, and in the early 1880's it was agreed that land north of the railway could be used for private housing. In June 1882 items dating back to the Celts were found during the excavations for the houses, while the following year further Celtic objects were discovered.

23. Chapel Street, from Brook Street, at the turn of the century. The Rose Inn was one of the many public houses in Basingstoke, often mistaken for the Rose and Crown in Church Street, which was also on a corner. Opposite the Rose, in Chapel Street, was the Brook Street Brewery, which was established in 1755 by the May family and closed down in 1950. The extensive complex of buildings was so large that it took over a year to demolish and clear the land for the Town Development Scheme in 1967; which included all the buildings in this picture.

24. Winchester Road in the late Victorian period, looking towards the town. The left side is now the site of the Camrose Football Ground, where the Basingstoke Football Club play their home matches, while further down the South Ham housing estate was built forty years ago. On the right the firm of Kelvin, Bottomley and Baird established their factory in 1937, later to become Smith's Industries. Due to the increase in road traffic in the 1920's along this road, it was decided to build a by-pass south of the town in 1931.

25. London Road, looking westward towards the town centre, about 1900. This was a well-photographed part of Basingstoke, its treelined road being a favourite spot for folk taking advantage of the Filmograph magazine cameras that were being sold at that time. The White Hart public house, in the centre, has been in business for over 250 years, its position outside the town centre preventing it from being demolished in the mass demolition of the 1960's. The left hand side was acquired for private houses, then in 1967 part of the land was used for the construction of the Police Station and Magistrate Courts.

26. Lower Wote Street, looking towards Station Hill in the 1890's. Mr. Soper's foundry was at the rear of the buildings on the left, while the first telephone exchange was fitted up in the upper room of Mr. Flux's shop at the turn of the century. The rear was later taken over by Mr. Hedges for his greenhouses, which he kept in conjunction with his shop, while further along Mr. Thomas opened up his cabinet making and upholstery business. William Stevens established a fish and chip shop among the shops here, but this had to close down and was demolished with the rest of the buildings in 1967.

27. The front of the Town Hall during preparations for Queen Victoria's Jubilee in 1887. The town celebrated with an assortment of events and functions, including an outdoor luncheon in front of the Town
Hall. The Queen had often stopped at Basingstoke in her special train, whilst travelling down to Osborne
House on the Isle of Wight. In more recent years Royalty has visited the town on several occasions, the
most recent being that of the Princess of Wales in 1986. In 1973 the Queen walked through the new shopping centre and opened the offices of the Automobile Association.

28. Chapel Street in the Edwardian days, showing the east side below Junction Road. This was undoubtedly the most attractive part of the town, as well as the oldest, with its fine 16th and 17th century houses. The demolition of these buildings during the period up to the Town Development Scheme caused much anguish among the local folk. This display of ivy was a common feature of local residences in those days, and although it caused weaknesses in the structure of some of the buildings, most people preferred the sight of the creeping plant, to the plain walls of their homes.

The Avenue, Winchester Rd. Basingstoke, 4047.

29. Pack Lane, Kempshott, some eighty years ago, when it was known as 'The Avenue'. Its abundance of trees from Winchester Road through to 'The White Gates' and beyond were popular for walks by families living in the area. It is only in the past thirty years that these tall trees have been felled by high winds and disease. In September 1961 a fungus struck many of the fine beeches and made them unsafe, so they had to be cut down. In the following January strong winds brought several crashing down, causing concern among the residents, so consequently others were removed.

30. Reading Road bridge during the widening of the railway for four tracks in 1904. It was decided that the right hand bridge was not strong enough to take the motor vehicles which were beginning to use the roads, so the left hand one was built. This part of the town was known as Northern Hill, but was later shortened to Norn Hill. Further down the hill, which is known as Reading Road, this was the Totterdown area of Basingstoke of Victorian times.

31. Lower Wote Street in the early years of this century, showing the area where the Basingstoke Canal Wharf was situated. The land to the left was acquired by George Casey for the construction of his Waldorf Cinema in 1935, this being his third cinema he had acquired since his arrival in Basingstoke in 1913. He died at the age of 63 in 1937. The Waldorf later became the ABC and then the Cannon, but was forced to close down early this year due to poor attendances.

WINTER   LONDON ROAD, PASINGSTOKE.

32. London Road during one of the harsh winters of the Edwardian period. The road was notorious for its snowdrifts due to the wind blowing the snow off the Basingstoke Common and being trapped up against the hedges on either side. One of the worst snowfalls occurred in April 1908 when nearly a foot of snow fell in a short time and then a sudden thaw resulted in the streets of Basingstoke being flooded, especially the lower part of the town.

33. London Road, near Eastrop Lane, at the turn of the century. The land to the right belonged to the Goldings estate, which became the War Memorial Park in 1921, although the land seen here was used for residential purposes. The motor car in the centre of the picture was one of the first to be used in Basingstoke. A letter to the Hampshire County Council in 1906 complained of children throwing stones at motorcars and asked for schools to point out to children the dangers of such a practice, but no action was ever taken.

34. The old Queen Mary's School in Worting Road at the turn of the century. Now part of the Basingstoke Technical College, it had its roots from the Holy Ghost Chapel school on the Liten Hill. In 1855 it was decided to transfer the school to Worting Road to a new site. Over the following years additions were made to the new building, a new schoolroom being added in 1874 and further classrooms and dormitories built some five years later. In 1894 a laboratory and workshop were also erected. By the end of the 19th century some 85 boys were being taught there. In 1960 a new Technical College was built on land opposite the school, at a cost of £211,450.

Sarum Hill, Basingstoke

35. Sarum Hill in Edwardian days, looking down towards the Flaxfield Road and Essex Road junctions. The roadside trees were a common feature around the town, but the Hampshire County Council decided that they were a danger to motor vehicles after the Motor Car Bill of 1903, which permitted traffic to travel up to 20 miles per hour, and many of them were removed. The railings which fronted so many of the front gardens were taken down and used to make armaments and ammunition during the Great War, as metal was in short supply.

36. The ruins of Basing House, at Old Basing village near Basingstoke, after excavations during the Edwardian period. Although the ruins are outside Basingstoke, the house was historically linked with the town, as most of the armoury and men used against the Marquis of Winchester and his men were based at Basingstoke. When the Marquis was finally captured by Oliver Cromwell, in October 1645, he was brought to Basingstoke and placed in the cellar of the Bell Inn in London Street for the night, before being transferred to the Tower of London.

37. Winchester Road in Edwardian days, looking towards Bramblys Grange. The houses on the right are still there, most of them over the years converted into offices. The large residence on the right was Brinkletts House, named after the Brinkletts Farm which was where the present car park is. The house in the centre of the picture became a shop belonging to Mr. J.W. Lester, a confectioner, in more recent years, then taken over by Mr. H.J. Ross, who later opened it up, in the 1960's, as a general store. It is now a takeaway restaurant.

38. Thornycrofts Works, along the Worting Road, at the turn of the century. This photograph was taken from the Waterworks site, which was opened in 1906 on the hill near the railway. The field in front of the factory was acquired in 1910 and laid out at a cost of £600, by the local Council, as the King George V's Playing Field. In the 1950's this field was used by the Basingstoke Skid Kids, a group of young cyclists, as their meeting place and cycle track. Part of the field was acquired for the Ring Road Roundabout at West Ham in the Town Development Scheme.

39. The interior of Burberry's factory at the rear of London Street, showing most of the staff working on the famous raincoats which Thomas Burberry produced. He came to Basingstoke in 1868 and opened up a small clothing firm in New Street, but as the business grew he moved to London Street. His examination of the local shepherds' all weather clothing brought about his invention of his 'Gabardine', a waterproof material from which he designed his 'Burberry' raincoat. He died in 1926, his two sons taking over the business. The firm moved from Basingstoke in the 1950's to concentrate its work in London.

40. Bramblys Grange Lane about 1910. This scene, from Winchester Road, was altered in 1939 when Bramblys Drive and Close houses were built in a half circular road from Penrith Road. The cottages on the right belonged to Bramblys Grange House, the home of Mr. Thornycroft, whose factory dominated Worting Road from 1898 until 1973. Both cottages and house were demolished to make way for the present Medical Centre. Much damage was done to the tall trees in the hurricane force winds of recent years.

41. Franklin's Antique shop in lower Church Street earlier this century. This fine old Tudor building stood on the corner of Church Street and Church Square, opposite St. Michael's Church. Like many of the other properties in the area it was badly damaged by the bombs that fell in August 1940 during the Second World War. One bomb caused a crater in the middle of Church Street and broke the water main underneath. As the water bubbled up to the surface one excited cyclist thought it was a puddle and ran straight into the crater, getting soaked up to his neck in the process.

42. Reading Road and Wote Street junction in early Edwardian days. In the distance is the Engineers Arms public house, which was established after the engineering firm of Wallis and Haslam opened in Station Hill in 1860. Basing Road and Reading Road passed on either side of the public house. In 1899 the British Water Trough Association presented the trough on the right to Basingstoke, and this remained there until 1967 when it was removed for the Town Development Scheme. The mass of trees which hid the River Loddon and Basingstoke Canal Wharf gradually disappeared in the following years.

43. A general scene of the Town Hall and Market Place in Edwardian times. To the left is Tyrrell's store which was demolished in the 1920's for the building of the Lloyds Bank, while the Tudor house next door was also pulled down, in 1961, for an extension to the bank. The Corn Exchange can be seen to the far right, in Wote Street, which was gutted by fire in 1925 and rebuilt. The clock tower on the Town Hall, built in 1887, was dismantled in late 1961 due to being unsafe. The actual Town Hall was used as Council offices until 1921 when the Goldings House in London Road was acquired for that purpose.

44. The Electric Theatre, off lower Wote Street, was one of the first cinemas to open in Hampshire, in October 1910. Built on the site of a swimming pool, the building enjoyed several years as being the town's only cinema, until the Grand Theatre was opened in the Wote Street Corn Exchange in 1913. Upon the opening of two other cinemas, the Plaza in Sarum Hill in 1925 and the Waldorf in lower Wote Street in 1935, the Electric was rebuilt in 1939 and called the Savoy. In August 1966 the Savoy was forced to close down due to the Town Development Scheme, and was demolished a few months later.

45. The Market Place in the Edwardian period, looking towards London Street. The van behind the large lamp-post belonged to Barton's Bakery of London Street. The lamp-post on the left was erected in 1903 in memory of the May family, who established the Brook Street Brewery in 1755. This structure was knocked down in the 1950's and never replaced. Most of the buildings in the Market Place have been demolished, although the distant ones, in London Street, are still there. The George Inn, dating from the 15th century, remains, although a recent planning application nearly saw its demise.

46. Hackwood Road in Edwardian times. This scene was taken near the London Road end, which has changed drastically in recent years. The houses on the left were demolished to make way for a new road, while the buildings on the right were pulled down for the construction of the Civic Offices in 1976. The original Pages Almshouses were on the left, until rebuilt in New Road in 1930. Established in 1802 by Joseph Page, they were again rebuilt further down New Road in 1975, to allow the construction of more residences for the elderly.

47. Soper's Almshouses in Chapel Street. Built in 1891 they were saved from demolition in 1904 during the widening of the railway due to an old mill being next to the Chapel Street bridge. John Burgess Soper was a popular character in the town, his foundry in Wote Street and his shop in the Market Place being busy places in the late Victorian period. He was a Councillor and became Mayor in 1888. Four years after he established the Chapel Street Almshouses he died at the age of 71, having celebrated his golden wedding anniversary a few years before. The Almshouses, like so many other buildings, were demolished in 1966.

48. The Mechanics Institute in New Street at the turn of the century. The Institute was originally established in Cross Street in 1841, but due to an increase in its membership it was able to move into a new building in 1869, erected at a cost of £1,200, and opened on 13th October of that year by Canon Charles Kingsley, the author of 'Water Babies'. The Institute's adult education programme was extensive and included lectures on most subjects. In 1928 the building was acquired for a Public Library, which was on the ground floor, and in 1930 the upper floor was used for a Museum.

49. Lower Wote Street in 1904, showing the old sheds of the timber yard kept by Mr. E.C. White. The area was once the wharf belonging to the Basingstoke Canal, but its closure in the late 19th century brought about the land being used for other purposes. In December 1890 a serious fire at Mr. White's steam saw-mills in the timber yard caused the destruction of some £2,000 worth of property. Mr. White died in 1924, and ten years later the yard was cleared of the old buildings. The land was later acquired for a bus station, while part of it was used for the New Market Square.

50. The Basingstoke Railway Station during alterations in 1904, when the lines between London and Southampton were increased from two to four. The railway was opened on 10th June 1839, when a party of directors travelled from London to Winchfield and formally opened the line from that station to Basingstoke. They were met along the line by crowds of cheering people, and on arriving at Basingstoke drank a toast to the future of the line. It is said that when goods trains began along the line three young teenage boys ran the business. Later on a man took their place.

51. Steam Dell Mill, off Reading Road, at the turn of the century. It was here that the original Waterworks were situated until 1905, when a break in the pipe caused a contamination which resulted in the deaths of some 15 people from typhoid. The Waterworks was closed down and a new one was set up at West Ham in 1906. In March 1906 claims by thirty people were made for compensation, the incident having caused a lot of bad feeling in the town. The young son of John Mares, the local clothing manufacturer, also died from the epidemic, and a plaque in memory of him was placed in May Place Hall.

S. Michael's Church, Basingstoke.

52. St. Michael's Church interior in the early Edwardian period. In 1908, shortly after Dr. H.W. Boustead took over as vicar of the church, the whole of the flooring in the nave and chancel was taken up and re-laid on a concrete foundation, while the seating on the ground floor of the church was entirely altered. Benches in the centre of the nave, for use of the poor, were removed. On 14th September 1938 fire destroyed most of the south aisle roof while water used by firemen ruined the organ. Within a year the restoration was complete and a new organ was fitted.

53. London Street about 1900, looking towards the Market Place. On the left is Mr. Jacob's leather shop, after whom the nearby alleyway was named. In more recent years the yard and offices in Mark Lane have been named after him. Opposite is the Red Lion Hotel and the Anchor Inn. The Red Lion was a popular coaching inn until the railway took away its transport business. Each coach had its own name, the Defiance, Eclipse, Magnet and the Age being a few of them that rode through the town.

54. The Congregational Church in London Street at the turn of the century. Originally known as the Independent Church, which used to have its hall in Cross Street, it became the Congregational and then the United Reform Church. This tall building was erected in 1800 and enlarged in 1860. May Place Hall, tucked away down a narrow lane on the right, was built in 1906 and enlarged in 1928; in recent years it has been acquired for offices. At the rear of the church a schoolroom was erected in 1872 and extended in 1888, which is now used for various activities.

55. Watson's Garage in lower Wote Street at the turn of the century. Their premises at no. 48 and 50 Wote Street were to see the many changes in motor vehicle design over the following sixty years until the area was demolished in 1966. The garage was agent for Vauxhall, Daimler, Lanchester, Jaguar and Land Rover, and had an extensive repairs department as well. As Wote Street was a busy thoroughfare there were several petrol pumps outside to cater for the consumption of fuel in those days.

56. Church Square junction with Mortimer Lane and Church Lane at the turn of the century. These buildings were destroyed by the German bombs in August 1940, during the Second World War, in which many people died. Church Lane used to go right up to Cross Street, but the construction of Timberlake Road in the 1960's led it to be diverted into Church Street. This part of Basingstoke was mainly used by business people, doctors and dentists, and the destruction of their homes in 1940 meant they had to find alternative accommodation.

57. The Mark Lane Forge at the turn of the century. Situated in the entrance to the local Police Station, off London Street, it had a series of owners, from John Lansley a century ago to George Long in the 1920's. When the 20th century began Edward Knight was the owner, and upon his death in 1904 his son carried on the business. With its hot, glowing fire, smoky atmosphere, and the sound of the heaving bellows, the local children found it a fascinating place. As the smithy shoed the horses so the ring of metal upon stone would ring out into London Street.

Basingstoke. Hackwood Road.

58. The thatched cottages in Hackwood Road in the early Edwardian days. This row of cottages stood near the Cliddesden Road junction, next to the Tollgate cottage in Hackwood Road. A row of shops and a car park now stands on the site. The Tollgate cottage was pulled down in 1929, the original gate being moved in 1861. Similar tollgates were also in London Road, Reading Road, Chapel Hill, and Winchester Road in the early 19th century, when money was taken to travel along those roads.

CHURCH ST. BASINGSTOKE.

59. Lower Church Street looking toward the town centre, about 1903. In 1901 the St. John's National School was opened, on the left of the picture, it having been a Sunday School since 1896. Enlarged to hold 130 boys and girls and 230 infants, the school remained there until 1966 when it had to close down for the Town Development Scheme when the whole area was demolished. The buildings opposite were not touched. The white building on the right was pulled down some forty years ago, part of which was the Harrow public house.

60. William Cannon's butcher's shop in London Street early this century. Mr. Cannon was a keen bowler and belonged to the Basingstoke Bowling Club, which used to hold its matches in the War Memorial Park. His shop was later acquired by Woolworths for the site of their store in 1921, and then by the Post Office in 1970. During the alterations in the 1920's remains of a medieval building were found between London Street and Southern Road, revealing many items of interest.

61. Thomas Burberry's store in Winchester Street just prior to the great fire of 17th April 1905, when some £30,000 worth of damage was done to the building and adjoining properties. Burberry's store was completely gutted, due to a shortage of water and a strong wind. The fire started accidently when a girl assistant knocked over an oil lamp while putting a display into one of the windows. Within 18 months the store was rebuilt.

62. Thomas Burberry's store in Winchester Street after its destruction by fire in 1905. It was ironic that 15 years before, in December 1890, another fire occurred in the shop window, as an assistant lit a gaslight with a taper. On that occasion a bucket of water was quickly fetched and thrown over the flames, resulting in the rest of the shop being saved. Mr. Burberry had other stores and warehouses in the town, as well as a factory and offices in London Street.

Station Hill, Basingstoke

63. Station Hill, looking down onto lower Wote Street, in Edwardian days, known to most folk as the 'steep hill that led to the railway station'. On one side of the road was Wallis and Steevens, an engineering firm, established in 1860, and Gerrish, Ames and Simpkins, the clothing manufacturer, built in 1878, on the other side. An assortment of shops and houses followed up the hill, which ranged from a grocer's, to a hairdresser's. In more recent years the west side was mainly acquired by Fred Smith's, the agricultural engineers, but in 1967 the road was demolished for the Town Development Scheme.

46082. BASINGSTOKE CANAL.

64. The Basingstoke Canal at Redbridge Lane, just off the London Road. This was one of the narrow stretches of the canal, which was built in the late 18th century, and caused problems for the barges bringing in their goods to the Basingstoke Wharf from the River Wey in Surrey. This area was known as Broadwater — not a very apt name at that point! As the canal passed the Basing House ruins, so it widened out. In 1897 a dredger accidently removed the clay puddling and caused the water to seep away at the Basingstoke end of the canal. In the 1930's the Greywell to Basingstoke section closed down.

65. The Methodist Chapel in Church Street prior to being moved to Cliddesden in 1904. The building was moved stone by stone to make way for a larger and grander church, which was built the following year. When the Wesleyan Chapel was erected in 1875 it was thought that the structure would be copious enough, but the population increase in Basingstoke brought about a larger congregation than was estimated. Even the construction of a new Methodist Church in Sarum Hill was not sufficient. (The Cliddesden Chapel has since been closed and sold as a residence.)

66. The opening of the new Methodist Chapel in Church Street on 9th March 1905. The site previously held another chapel, but this was dismantled and moved to Cliddesden village, having been erected in Church Street in 1875. The new Church Street chapel was built by a local builder, Mr. John Harris of Basing Road, while the architects were Gordon and Gunton of Blomfield Street in London. The opening ceremony was carried out by Lady Marshall, the wife of the Sheriff of the City of London. One year previously, on 30th June 1904, the stone-laying ceremony was carried out by the Earl of Portsmouth and Bishop Hoss of the U.S.A.

67. Sarum Hill Methodist Church at the time of the Great War. Built in 1902 as the Primitive Methodist Chapel, at a cost of £4,643, it was designed to hold 580 seats. A small cottage alongside was built for the caretaker. In 1970 the church was demolished after a new Trinity Church was erected further down the hill, the old site being used for the construction of an office block. The Church Hall, which was attached to the rear of the old church, remained in place until 1984.

68. The Orangery in the Goldings private estate, off London Road. This became part of the War Memorial Park in 1921 when the estate became acquired for that purpose by several business men. The emphasis in those days was to keep the gardens as attractive as possible, and the greenhouse in the background was used to produce the necessary plants and flowers for the park. After the Second World War the gardens disappeared, with the greenhouse, to make way for a bowling green, but this was also removed in later years. It is now the site of the new Civic Offices extension.

69. Miles and son's boot and shoe repair shop on the corner of Chapel Street and Junction Road in Edwardian days. The display of materials used or sold was a common feature in those days, and in this case it was strips of leather placed on the outside walls. In later years this shop was taken over as a tobacconist's by Mr. F. Cripps, who later on expanded the business into a newsagent's. Junction Road was built in 1871 to allow traffic into Station Hill and to the railway station, from Chapel Street, to avoid the round trip down to Brook Street and back up Station Hill. This area was demolished in 1967.

70. The Black Dam earlier this century. The area, which consisted of four ponds and a large expanse of marshland, was a favourite place for children to catch their tadpoles, many of which ended up at the local schools for nature lessons. It was feared that the construction of the Basingstoke bypass in 1931 would affect the wildlife, but the road was made north of the area. But the Town Development road system of the 1960's was not so kind, and Basingstoke lost a large section of the ponds and land for the new A30 and the M3 motorway.

sleyan Ch. Basingstoke. New Organ opened. 5.7.06

71. The interior of the Church Street Methodist Church after the new organ was installed on 5th July 1906. Just over a year before the church had been officially opened during the ministry of Reverend H.J. Chapman. 34 years later a German bomb did considerable damage to the inside of the church and it was not until September 1950 that the building was restored and re-opened for worship. The church was forced to close in October 1965 and later demolished to make way for the new shopping centre.

Recreation Ground, Basingstoke

Buckland's series, Basingstoke

72. Fairfields Recreation Ground before the Great War, with Fairfields School in the background. The gardens were opened by John May, the local benefactor, in 1902, and in later years a bowling green and tennis courts were added. When the War Memorial Park was opened in 1921 the bandstand was moved from Fairfields to a new site in the middle of the park.

73. Winchester Street in Edwardian days, after Thomas Burberry had rebuilt his 'Emporium' after the fire of 1905. The store on the left hand corner, adjoining New Street, belonged to Mr. Ody, who later moved his grocery business across the road to premises now occupied by the Halifax Building Society. Lansley's butcher's shop, on the right, was established in 1837 and closed down in 1962. The shop was on the corner of Victoria Street, which was a narrow track until 1899 when it was widened.

The Cottage Hospital, Basingstoke

74. The Cottage Hospital on the corner of Southern Road and Hackwood Road. Built in 1879 from subscriptions raised by local businessmen and residents, it was extended over the following years, with an X-ray and ophthalmic department added in 1921. By 1911 it had 18 beds and at the end of that year had given aid to 144 patients. In the 1930's a series of carnivals raised sufficient money for the construction of an out-patients department after the Second World War. The opening of the Basingstoke Hospital off the Aldermaston Road, in 1974, led to the Cottage Hospital being disused for general medical purposes.

75. Reverend Harry Wilson Boustead, vicar of St. Michael's Church from 1905 to 1936. He was probably one of the most controversial vicars of all time, due to his many outspoken remarks on various local topics. It is legend that he locked the church doors on the Mayor of Basingstoke, once, who was forced with his Corporation to use a side door to enter the church during the Civic Parade and Service of that year. Born in 1858 in London, Reverend Boustead died in 1942, aged 84.

Eastrop Lane, Basingstoke.

76. Eastrop Church in Eastrop Lane about the year 1910. This lane was commonly known as 'Lovers Lane' as so many young couples used to stroll along its leafy track in those days. In 1932 the lane was widened and surfaced as a by-pass road for traffic wanting to travel from south to north of the town and vice-versa, resulting in the Eastrop Bridge, which used to span the Basingstoke Canal, being partly demolished. In 1966 its brickwork was discovered by workmen while digging a trench by the side of the road. Eastrop Church was rebuilt in 1886, while services were held at the Basingstoke Town Hall.

77. The Town Hall, erected in 1832 to replace a similar building that had stood there since 1657, consisted of a reading
room, justice and council rooms, with a retiring room next
door. On the upper floor there was a spacious hall, often used
for dances, and town clerk's and borough surveyor's offices.
The cost of the site and its erection totalled some £10,000. In
1887 a new clock tower was built over the original one at the
sole expense of the mayor, John May, on the occasion of the
Golden Jubilee of Queen Victoria. This tower was dismantled in 1961 after being declared unsafe.

C.C. High School, Basingstoke.

T.H.
B.

78. The Basingstoke High School for Girls, at Crossborough Hill, shortly after being opened in September 1912. It was originally established in the ivy-clad Brook House in Brook Street in 1908, but the school outgrew the building, so at a cost of £2,000 for the site and £7,000 for the construction the new premises were built. Over the years extensions and additions were made, including a large swimming pool which was built in 1961. Ten years later the school was renamed after a previous schoolmistress, Harriet Costello.

79. The cattle pens in Vyne Road, where animals waiting to attend the Cattle Market were kept. These were just below Phoenix Park Terrace, the site now being a car park. The Cattle Market, in front of the Railway Station, was established in 1873 by Hugh Raynbird and his two sons. In December of that year they held a fat stock sale, then ran a series of monthly cattle sales. These proved so popular that eventually they were held every Wednesday. The Cattle Market closed down in May 1966, and both pens and market buildings were pulled down.

80. The Market Place during the Great War, during construction work for Barclays Bank. The building was originally the Angel Inn, an old coaching inn dating back to the 16th century, but it closed down in 1866 and was converted into shops. A café was opened up in an upper room and was called the Angel Café, in memory of the inn. At the rear of the inn was the Assembly Rooms, a large arched structure in whose upper rooms Jane Austen, the novelist, used to visit for dancing lessons.

81. Winton Square during the Great War. The Wheatsheaf Hotel, on the left, has seen many changes to its property, with different entrances being made over the past two centuries, and internal alterations in recent years; while the rear has seen the disappearance of its car park and garages for the construction of offices. During the 19th century the fields behind the hotel were used for the Michaelmas Fair, at which the annual hiring of labourers took place. The shops to the right of the picture were built in 1907 to replace old delapidated buildings.

7th North Staffords.

82. The 7th North Staffords resting by the roadside at Basingstoke during training in 1915. They were based temporarily on the fields outside the town, prior to being transported to France to fight the Germans during the Great War. A large part of the Basingstoke Common was used by various military groups to encamp while waiting to travel down to Southampton to be shipped across the English Channel.

83. West Ham House and its grounds during the Great War, when the residence was used as a hospital for wounded soldiers. The estate consisted of some 200 acres, including park and grounds, farmland, lodges, several cottages, and woodland. The land was acquired by the commercial vehicle manufacturers of Thornycrofts for leisure purposes, and in the years after the Second World War many sporting activities took place there. The Town Development Scheme involved the acquisition of the grounds for industrial purposes, while the farmland was used for an entertainment complex.

84. Some of the many troops that were encamped on the fields around Basingstoke during the Great War. Most of the soldiers were put under canvas prior to being transported to France to fight against the Kaiser. Troops were also housed in various halls in the town, while the presence of so many 'strangers' in the area scared some women, their absence being noticed at the church services in Basingstoke. It was during the war that many of these women offered their help in the fields and factories as so many men had been called up.

85. Delivery of goods to Cliddesden Road houses by the International Stores van. This was a regular service not only by that store, whose shop was in the Market Place, but by most of the other local grocery businesses. Other shops, such as baker's, butcher's, and hardware stores, also supplied a delivery service, but this all came to an end in the years after the Second World War, when labour and petrol became expensive.

86. Flaxfield Road and Mortimer Lane corner, prior to the left hand side buildings being demolished. The land was acquired as a builders yard by G.W. Oliver. In recent years the firm closed down and private houses have been built on the site. The area was originally meadowland where flax was grown, this being a blue-flowered plant cultivated for its seeds in the making of linseed, and for its stem in the making of textile fibre. In the 1880's part of the area was built on by a builder from Essex, who called most of the roads after that part of England.

87. London Street, looking eastward from the Market Place, during the Great War. The shop on the right was Kingdon's ironmongery business, which was known as Kingdon and Lodwidge after Mr. Kingdon took over the business in 1886. Mr. Kingdon died in 1901 but the family continued to run the business until it was taken over by Carpenter's in recent years, by which time it had moved from the Market Place to the new shopping centre. It was in this part of London Street that several of the multiple stores opened up in the 1920's and 1930's, such as Woolworths and Boots the Chemists.

88. Vyne Road/Queen Mary's Avenue junction about seventy years ago. In the 1880's much of the land north of Basingstoke was acquired for residential purposes and Vyne Road was one of several roads built at that time. A pathway which used to follow on across the right hand field to Sherborne St. John village was the scene of the 'Cornfield Murder' of 1924. In 1939 the Queen Mary's School was built in the field, while the avenue (right) was constructed in 1946.

89. Crowds outside Lanham's store in Winchester Street, during the annual sales, in 1914. Edgar Lanham acquired Thomas Burberry's store in 1914, this being the 'Emporium' built after the great fire of 1905. In 1964 it became Thomas Wallis's, who held it for ten years until Maples took it over. Last year Kingsbury's moved in, to sell mainly furniture. In Lanham's time the store sold nearly every household item that was needed.

90. The Thornycroft Band in 1920. Basingstoke had quite an assortment of bands at the turn of the century, an entertainment which the population of the town enjoyed. Without any radio or television in those days, people made their own entertainment, and listening to or playing in a band was a way to pass the time. In Basingstoke there were the K Company Volunteer Band, the Railway Temperance Band, Mechanic's Institute Band, North Hants Ironworks Band, Basingstoke Silver Band, Salvation Army Band and the Primitive Methodist Band as well.

91. The east side of upper Church Street in the 1920's. The outfitting shop of Horace Carey was established in 1924, next to Mr. Brickell's bakery. Mr. Carey was a close friend of George Willis, who began the Museum in New Street, and their interests in the fauna and flora of the area led them to visit the various woods and fields around the town. Mr. Brickell and his wife escaped with their lives in September 1927 when their shop and bakery were badly damaged by fire. The shop was later taken over by Henry Thornton and called Southwells Bakery. It is now the office of the 'Basingstoke Gazette' newspaper.

92. Wote Street, near Potters Lane, when the Post Office was there. Robert Cottle established a Post Office in the town, in the early 19th century, at his store in Winchester Street, but upon his death in 1859 it was moved to Wote Street. In 1880 it was transferred to premises opposite, where it remained until 1925, when it again moved, to New Street. In 1970 it moved to its present site, in London Street, after Woolworth's store moved down to the new shopping centre.

93. Worting Village in the early 1920's before the tyre retread factory of Blue Peter was established there. Two brothers, Captain P. Kent and Commander J. Kent, called the firm Auto Tyre Services, after setting up business in the small village, but in later years it was renamed Blue Peter Retreads. Two serious fires, in 1932 and 1933, caused much damage, but by the time the Second World War had broken out they were in full production, although the destruction of the Far East rubber plantations by the Japanese caused problems. The firm closed down in 1973.

94. The view from the Town Hall clock tower looking down on Church Street earlier this century. St. Michael's Church, in the centre of the picture, was mainly built in the 16th century, but the pinnacles on top of the tower were not completed until 1879. In that same year the churchyard was improved as well. The corner of Cross Street and Church Street (facing, left) was demolished in the 1940's, while the main section on the right was pulled down in the 1960's for the new shopping centre.

95. Upper Church Street, before the fire of 1935 swept through the premises on the right. In 1930 Mr. William Aston acquired the old furniture warehouse known as the Little Dustpan and converted it into a drapery arcade, which included an aviary. On the night of 29th August 1935 a fire started in the shop and spread quickly throughout the premises. It was ironic that Thomas Burberry, whose store was consumed by fire some thirty years before, had a warehouse immediately opposite. Further down the road, on the left, was Longley's drapery store whose name is still retained in an antique furniture shop.

Basingstoke
Butchers' Outi
1925

96. The Basingstoke butchers' annual outing in 1925 - one of the many char-à-banc trips of those days after the Great War. With this type of transport it was a case of once you were in your seat you were, more or less, there for the rest of the journey, and at the mercy of the elements until you got the rear hood up! There were at least a dozen butchers in Basingstoke at the turn of the century, including Holly's and Lansley's. Griffin Bros. in Church Street, who were established in 1896, became popular for their 'Basingstoke pork sausages', as well as being cooked meat specialists.

97. An aerial picture of London Street taken between the wars. Upon the cessation of the Great War many private air pilots established aerial photography businesses and the consequences were that most towns had aeroplanes flying about taking photographs from all angles. This picture, with the Congregational Church in the centre, was one of many taken by one of those firms.

Winchester Street Basingstoke

98. Winchester Street in the 1920's. The small square building on the left was the original offices of the solicitors Lamb, Brooks and Bullock, but in 1937 the land was cleared for the building of the Montague Burton shop, which was opened by Austin Burton in 1938. Above the premises were offices, one floor being used as the Luciana Billiard Club. Marks and Spencers store opened their building in 1934, their frontage being on the far left of the picture. Opposite was the large store of Lanhams, which was previously Burberry's Emporium.

99. The scene after the Grand Cinema fire in May 1925. The Grand, opened by George Casey in June 1913, was also used as a theatre, and at the time was showing a performance of 'Tit for Tat'. Just after midnight on 16th May a policeman saw smoke rising from the large building and raised the alarm. The Basingstoke Fire Brigade, helped by Thornycrofts' private brigade, fought the blaze but the building was gutted. Damage was estimated at £4,000 with the roof destroyed and only the four outer walls remaining. It was later rebuilt to a similar design.

100. The Holy Ghost Chapel ruins before the gravestones were removed and the area landscaped. Built in the 15th century by the Holy Ghost Guild the land was used as a burial ground after the Interdict of 1208-1214 would not allow burials on consecrated ground. In 1817 some labourers found the remains of an ancient church, while digging between the chapel and the old schoolhouse, including a stone effigy of a Knight Templar. As this order was abolished in 1312 it was evidently of great age.

101. Sir Alan Cobham talking to sightseers at Popley Fields, north of Basingstoke, in the mid-1920's. Born in 1894 he became a well-known air pilot through his long-distance flights to various countries. In 1926 he flew from London to Cape Town and back, and to Australia and back. In that same year he received the honour of the Knight Commander of the order of the British Empire. He flew to various places around Britain, including Basingstoke, to give advice and encouragement to youngsters wanting to join the Royal Air Force and fly. He was in the R.A.F. during the Great War.

102. Park Prewett Mental Hospital, to the north of the town, was built in 1913, the site having been purchased by the Hampshire County Council in 1902. The huge complex of buildings was built on part of the Park Prewett Farm, during which a section of the old Roman Road from Silchester to Winchester was revealed. In 1957 and 1981 fire severely damaged part of the central buildings. In 1975 Princess Alexandra officially opened the Basingstoke and District Hospital, built to the east of the Park Prewett Hospital.

103. The scene at the bottom of Wote Street in January 1926 after a heavy fall of snow. The Barge Inn, on the right, was an old established public house dating back to the construction of the Basingstoke Canal in the 1780's. It was one of the many drinking houses that were demolished in 1966 for the Town Development Scheme. Brook Street, which runs through the centre of this picture, was aptly named, for it was through here that the River Loddon used to flow.

104. The interior of the workshops at Messrs. Thornycrofts in the late 1920's. The firm's spacious works on the Worting Road was mainly concerned in the manufacture of commercial vehicles, but during the First and Second World Wars it produced a large quantity of military vehicles. John I. Thornycrofts and Co. Ltd. was established in Basingstoke in 1898 and three years later became incorporated. Over the years many types of vehicles were made, from steam vans to double decker buses. In 1928 John Thornycroft died and his elder son, also John, took over as company chairman. The business was sold in 1973 and leased to Eaton Transmissions Ltd.

105. The Basingstoke by-pass during construction in 1930, at the London Road end. Since the arrival of the motorcar Basingstoke had suffered the onslaught of vehicles charging through the town centre, causing clouds of dust and chaos. The by-pass cost some £55,000 including compensation to landowners, the construction of a bridge at Viables over the Alton Light Railway (which was about to close down) and the connection to the Winchester and London roads at each end. Part of the by-pass went through the Basingstoke Common and Harrow Way.

106. Worting Road in the 1930's, looking west from the Alton Light Railway bridge. The tall trees on the right belonged to the West Ham estate, many of which are still there. The houses on the left were built by the local Council in 1930 in conjunction with the Housing Act of that year. Eight houses were erected (known as the South Ham Scheme) for rehousing people displaced from Victoria Street and Worting Bottom, where certain properties were demolished. In the following years the nearby fields of South Ham Farm were also built upon, creating a large housing estate.

107. Cross Street/Church Street junction in pre-war days. When Mr. Appelbee's shop was demolished in 1946 two small unglazed drug cups were found in the wall beside the chimney breast, dating back to the 18th century. The site was never built on and remained waste land until Cross Street was widened out at that point about fifteen years later. Cross Street received its name from the days when the cattle crossed from the fields at Worting Road to the slaughterhouse in Wote Street.

108. A discarded combine harvester, a fallow field, and a distant view of Basingstoke. Such was the scene before the housing development invaded the countryside around the town. Although Basingstoke's development began in the late Victorian period, it was not until 1909 that the Local Government Board thought about a town planning scheme for the area. The local Medical Officer of Health was asked to submit his report on Basingstoke, but three years later he admitted that investigations were still being carried out as 'progress is somewhat slow'.